FLYING CROOKED

A STORY OF
ACCEPTING CANCER

Jan Michael

· · ·

FLYING
crooked

GREYSTONE BOOKS
Douglas & McIntyre Publishing Group
Vancouver/Toronto/Berkeley

05 06 07 08 09   5 4 3 2 1

Greystone Books
A division of Douglas & McIntyre Ltd.
2323 Quebec Street, Suite 201
Vancouver, British Columbia
Canada v5t 4s7

Library and Archives Canada Cataloguing in Publication
Michael, Jan, 1947–
Flying crooked : a story of accepting cancer / Jan Michael.

ISBN-13: 978-1-55365-130-7   ISBN-10: 1-55365-130-8

1. Michael, Jan, 1947– —Health.
2. Breast—Cancer—Patients—Biography. I. Title.
RC280.B8M524 2005   362.196'99449'0092   C2005-900938-1

Library of Congress information is available upon request

Published in Great Britain in 2004 by Mainstream
Publishing Company (Edinburgh) Ltd.
First published in the Netherlands in 2003 by Uitgeverij De Geus

Jacket and interior design by Jessica Sullivan
Jacket photograph ©Melanie Acevedo/Firstlight
Printed and bound in Canada by Friesens
Printed on acid-free paper that is forest-friendly (100% post-
consumer recycled paper) and has been processed chlorine-free
Distributed in the U.S. by Publishers Group West

We gratefully acknowledge the financial support of the Canada
Council for the Arts, the British Columbia Arts Council, and the
Government of Canada through the Book Publishing Industry
Development Program (BPIDP) for our publishing activities.

For Paul, with love

Flying Crooked

The butterfly, a cabbage-white,
(His honest idiocy of flight)
Will never now, it is too late,
Master the art of flying straight,
Yet has—who knows so well as I?—
A just sense of how not to fly:
He lurches here and here by guess
And God and hope and hopelessness.
Even the aerobatic swift
Has not his flying-crooked gift.

ROBERT GRAVES

FLYING CROOKED

Think little of thy flesh: blood, bones and a skin;
a pretty piece of knit and twisted work, consisting
of nerves, veins and arteries; think no more of
it than so. As for thy life, consider what it is: a wind;
not one constant wind neither, but every moment
of an hour let out, and sucked in again.

MARCUS AURELIUS, *Meditations*

The next morning, almost a whole day after the operation, I woke up and was happy. It was a pure happiness, the kind that comes only rarely. A happiness that seeps through your skin and your eyes and your nostrils, then creeps along your tissues and veins and arteries till it suffuses your heart and soul, and all of you is one, and all of you is happiness. Life is simple then.

It was a morning in February. The sky was gunmetal gray turning lighter, not a hint of blue, not a tree twisting in the wind. A long window ran alongside my bed.

Dawn was rising from the night. Streetlights were still on. I heard the soft shoes of the night nurse approach and turned my head slowly toward the young man. He smiled. He squatted to examine my drain, then stroked my hand. I'd met him already in the night when he'd come to check the drain from the wound, had soothed my pain, and sent me back to sleep. He put a thermometer in my ear.

Not everything was gray that happy morning. My sheets gleamed white and the blankets were softly cream. Spikes of grape hyacinths on the windowsill were taking on their deep blue color as the dawn came up; beside them, yellow tulips, just opening, still rigid, then a mixed jumble of red roses, blue irises, and more yellow tulips, all as bright as in a child's painting of sun and sky. I felt the nurse's breath on my cheek as he removed the thermometer. A touch on my head and he was gone. I never looked away from the sky. It was lightening now with flakes of snow.

I was happy and warm and safe. Nothing mattered but this, here, now, me the bed the flowers the sky the snow. If this was all, it was enough.

"I HAVE TO CHANGE your dressings." The day nurse drew the curtains round my bed and fussed with metal dishes and gauze and padding.

I knew what to expect. Six years before, on holiday in Gozo, Simon and I had gone to the museum behind the cathedral in the old island citadel. On the upper floor hung a gallery of paintings, each one of St. Agatha, patron saint of the cathedral; St. Agatha, tortured in a brothel by the Romans. Her final indignity: the cutting off of her breasts, first one then another. The paintings showed every moment in gaudy detail.

A soldier, bulky in his armor, wielded shears from the side that sliced through the flesh, leaving it bleeding and raw.

St. Agatha's eyes were cast up to heaven, in mute acceptance. I had felt sick. I'd left and waited outside for Simon.

"This may hurt a little."

I gazed over the nurse's head and gasped as she ripped plaster from the side of the gauze jacket that covered the dressing. She took hold of the large pad and lifted it.

So far so good. "I'd like to see." I struggled to sit up.

"No." She looked alarmed. "Not today. Leave it for another day. Rest today."

I was prepared for the stump. "I want to."

She sighed and moved her arm away so that it was no longer shielded.

"But . . . " the words choked in my mouth. "That's really neat." One side of me was breastless now, scooped out even. But the skin was folded over in a line that reached from my breastbone to my back. There was bruising but no blood, no raw flesh, just a long zipperlike wound. "I'm no worse than a sewn-up teddy bear!"

The news of my cancer had spread quickly, and that was fine. Friends came round. Hannah came with three-year-old Sophie and handed me a bottle of champagne—so we could enjoy lunch, she said.

"Stop work now," she said, handing me the post from the doormat. I slit open the top envelope:

I've just returned from lighting a candle in church for you.

I passed the card over to Hannah, my eyes watering.

"Whoo!" She swallowed, too, and slung an arm round my shoulders.

"And others have said they're praying for me, people I never thought were religious. I've never dared say that," I said.

"Why not?"

"Dunno really. Intrusive? I'm probably too inhibited."

"What a relief," she said, and squeezed my shoulder. "I've been praying for you." Unusual for her; she normally communicated through jokes.

"Oh, you!" I laughed through watery eyes. "I feel a fraud, though, all this attention. I'm fine. It's not as if I feel ill."

"Yeah, right. You've just got cancer. No big deal. Come on, champagne."

As they were leaving, Sophie, who'd had the odd sip from my glass, solemnly presented me with a straggly looking teddy bear "to sleep with you." We christened him at once: Thomas Percival Kieboom Bear. Tom for short.

When one is dying, one is much too busy
to think about death. All one's organism is
devoted to breathing.

ITALO SVEVO, *The Confessions of Zeno*

Simon burst into the ward after supper, stripping off coat, jacket, jumper as he came. "Hello, gorgeous! It's so *hot* in here," chucking them on the floor and pushing them into the corner with his foot. He had brought a heavy bunch of bananas that had yet to ripen, a basket of mandarins going dry, two pots of his favorite yogurt, and some books.

"Shall I read to you? Would you like me to massage your feet? Sorry I couldn't be here yesterday. Did Marie come? How about some tea? Look, I've brought a thermos of chamomile tea for you." He was pouring as he talked. "Well?"

"Well what?" I was beaming. He was as infuriating as a loud, clumsy puppy, and it cheered my heart to see him. My ex. We'd fallen in love years before, after a messy divorce on his side and a breakup on mine. We'd eventually moved in together and, after six years of disastrously irritating one another by how we lived, had agreed to split. The affair had lasted longer, but for some time now it had been no more than an easy, affectionate friendship. We'd never lost that. He'd come to some of my appointments with the specialists; Marie, my oldest friend, who'd introduced me to Simon, to others. Some I'd gone to alone.

"Shall I read to you?" Simon repeated. "I've brought some light reading: *Winnie the Pooh.*" My favorite childhood book.

Tears pricked at my eyelids. I seemed to have no skin left between me and my emotions. "Yes, in a moment. Just talk to me for now. Tell me how your trip went."

I looked at him curiously. He was blushing.

He'd had a great time, he said. Up in the mountains in Turkey, walking alone. He'd met only a couple of other walkers. He moved swiftly on.

DR. HUIZINGA, the surgeon, had sketched a diagram of my breast and slid it across his desk to Simon and me. "One tumor is close to the nipple, the other is over the right side, and the third is between them, so the whole breast will have to come off."

Bile rushed up into my throat. I swallowed it down. Then, almost miraculously, I felt swamped by a wave of resignation and I relaxed.

"We'll be cleaning out the armpit, of course."

"The armpit?" I asked, shocked out of my acceptance. "Is that really necessary?"

"Yes." He was firm. "We'll clear out the lymph glands in the armpit and examine them for cancer."

"And not put them back," I muttered.

"Quite."

"But it's my writing arm. I can't do without it. What about it being sore afterward and swelling up? Our biology teacher at school had it done, and her arm was useless."

"In the 1950s, was that? Techniques have improved somewhat since then. Your arm will be fine. You'll be able to use it, no problem."

"Is that a promise?"

He didn't skip a beat. "Yes."

"And it's you who'll operate?" I wanted to trust. Get a good surgeon, I'd been told. They cut cleanly and didn't spread the cancer cells about. Ask—if you dare—how often they've done the operation in the past year.

"Yes." He paused. "Then your left breast. We'll do a lumpectomy on that side."

"Why?" Simon this time, checking for me. "What's wrong with it?"

"There's a lump there."

"I know," I said, "but you don't think it's malignant. Why operate on a healthy breast?" It was all there was left to protest about.

"It could become malignant." His patience didn't waver.

"But . . ."

"Look, if you prefer, I can take off the whole breast."

I burst out laughing. "The whole . . . ? What?"

"For symmetry." He looked defensive, Simon startled.

"Symmetry?" I parroted.

"Some women like it because it evens them up." Now he was laughing too. Simon looked nervous.

"The hell they do!" I touched my left breast protectively. "I'll only have one left. I don't want to lose that too."

He then sent me for aspirations. Picked up the phone and arranged it. "In half an hour?"

Simon said he'd ring Marie and stay meanwhile. He'd been a star coming with me to the surgeon when Marie couldn't.

WE SAT ON PLASTIC chairs that were molded to fit no one. Simon looked wrong in these surroundings, so clinical and tidy. Not that Marie would have looked any better with her large frame, always glowing with good health. The tenth white coat who emerged from the corridor behind us was the pathologist.

"Does it hurt?" I asked him as we walked down the corridor. I didn't catch his name when he introduced himself. Shy and in his late fifties though.

He looked sideways at me. "I don't know." He sounded gloomy.

"You don't know?" I exclaimed.

"I've never had it done."

"Oh. Well, what about the women you've done it to?"

He shrugged. "Some say it hurts, others say it doesn't."

Very like Eeyore he was.

"Look," he said in some exasperation, as I suppose I went on looking at him in dread, "I can deaden your breasts for you, but I'll be going in three times for the aspiration: twice on one side, then once on the other, and to deaden them I'll have to go in once on either side, and they tell me that that injection hurts too. It's up to you. Would you get up on the bed, please?"

We were in the treatment room. Test room, I should perhaps say. Pathology department. He busied himself at the counter, his back to us.

"What's the maximum number of seconds it'll take each time?" I asked.

"Ten."

I glanced at Simon. He sat on the chair alongside and looked back. He seemed pale, but that might have been the fluorescent strip above our heads, bleaching all color from his face. "OK. No local anesthetic." I could feel myself grinning manically. Amazing what adrenaline can do.

"Do you enjoy your work?" I asked, making small talk as if this was some social occasion.

"I don't know," Eeyore answered.

"You mean she's your first patient?" Simon, rallying, pretending to be shocked.

"Of course not." He checked the syringe; it looked big enough for a horse. "It's just that I'm the first to see the cancer confirmed."

In went the first needle. I grabbed Simon's hand. "Ten," I said out loud, "nine, eight . . . seven," he joined in loudly, "six, five, four . . . " At "three" the pathologist removed the needle from my flesh. It wasn't so bad. Three times.

"I'm going next door to check that I've got enough," he said. "Rest there for a minute or two, then you can get up and dress."

When he returned, he busied himself with his back to us once more.

"Have you?" I asked.

"Have I what?" He was clattering away with the instruments.

"Got enough?"

"Yes."

"When will you know what the results imply?" I asked to his bent back, imagining three days or maybe twenty-four hours only, or perhaps eight hours, it was unlikely to be less than three.

"Oh," muttered Eeyore, "I have a clear idea already."

"If you have a clear idea," I said from the slab, hand on my breast, "may I ask what it is?"

"It's awkward."

"So they're malignant."

He sighed. "Yes, the bigger ones on the right. The one on the left may not be."

Marie was waiting outside when we came out. She stood quickly. Simon muttered to her and they followed me as I walked quickly out into the cold air and gulped it in.

We walked home, more or less in silence.

Cancer: death. You can't help making the jump. Marie had dark shadows under her eyes and was subdued, unlike her usual self; her mother had died of breast cancer relatively recently. Death didn't matter, I thought, watching my feet hit the pavement in turn, it was OK, I'd had a great life. Fine. We can't all live into old age. I was buoyed up with energy, I could cope, I knew I could.

Oh God!

I slid the key into the front door, turned to the left, unlocked it: actions done a hundred times before, different now, oddly momentous. Post on the mat. We all bent for it. "Ouch!" our heads banged. Marie giggled nervously. So then did I. "Here," she handed me the small pile.

On the top envelope, printed clearly in bold: OHRA INSURANCE: Funeral policy: have you made your arrangements yet?

Laughter poured out. Tears poured out. "Whiskey!" Simon headed for the kitchen and poured out three glasses, neat.

After that, I was wired. I made phone calls. Simon kept our whiskey glasses topped up. Marie put on water to feed us with pasta, but I wanted to go out to dinner. I couldn't sit still. I couldn't just stay at home, I had to move. "Let's ring Hannah, or Connie and Peter, see if they can come too."

And that's what we did. I drank a lot, we all drank a lot. They got drunk while I stayed sober and sharp, every nerve in my body alert to the tastes of the food, to my friends, to the smells in the air.

Death could drop from the dark
As easily as song.
ISAAC ROSENBERG,
"Returning, we hear the larks"

A card arrived. Taking it from its envelope, I read the words first: "Prayers, kisses, and love from Helen."

Tears prickled as they always seemed to be doing at the moment. I turned the card over to look at the picture: a tulip. From left to right, in three stages: upright, drooping, shedding its petals—dying. Guffawing, I stuck it to the side of my computer to keep me company.

I took it that evening when Simon and I went round to see friends, Katherine and Joshua, both young doctors who answered every question I could think of to throw at them.

I wanted to know everything. I needed to know worst-case scenarios: it was my coping mechanism. And they were brilliant. Not once did they tell me to deal with *x* when it happened, or that *y* might not happen at all. They answered everything straightforwardly.

"Hah!" exclaimed Joshua, looking at the card. "Friends of mine had their first baby recently," he said. "I was houseman at the hospital and couldn't get away to see them so I sent a card, one I'd picked up at a secondhand bookshop. It was of a woman in the 1950s, fur coat, padded shoulders, pushing a high pram; beside her, walking proudly, the father; in the pram, a piglet wearing a frilly bonnet. Just the thing, I thought. I wrote to the baby:'Dear Sam, welcome. I hope you aren't as much of a shock to your parents as this one'—and I sent it.

"A week later I heard from another friend that the baby had Down's syndrome. I rushed out, bought a huge bunch of flowers, and went straight round. When they came to the door, I apologized, I didn't know, I would never have sent such a stupid, tactless card if I had, and if they never wanted to speak to me again, I'd understand. They pulled me inside and hugged me.'Don't be daft,'they said. They said my card had been the only thing that whole first week that had made them laugh."

Exactly.

Simon attached a cardboard arrow to the card, below the picture of the tulips, and wrote: "How I'm feeling today."

"Now we shan't all have the bother of asking you how you are when you're in hospital," he said. "All you have to do is move the arrow."

Which I did.

IN A CURIOUS WAY, it's as if you're ill for other people. It's as if you're their sickness conductor, as well as their death conductor. Ringing friends and family to tell them about the cancer, I was the one doing the comforting and reassuring.

I got into the habit of asking them if they had some wine handy, asking them to toast me for luck. I brought up the subject of death to preempt their inhibitions. Spontaneously and innocently at first; later on, aware of what I was doing. By mentioning the supposedly unmentionable, it was possible to have wonderful conversations, and their reactions then gave me strength.

MA RANG AGAIN, from Madeira, where my parents had retired. She was still a bit weepy, but not as bad as when I'd originally told her. "We've done our weeping and wailing and gnashing of teeth," she said, and I could hear her smile through snuffles. She wanted to come over, but I put her off and sensed she was relieved. She was old and tired, and Amsterdam was hardly Madeira. She could barely walk and hated the cold. Better she and my father stayed where they were. Simon and Marie, both of whom they had met, promised to ring them regularly.

"Oh!" The room the nurse had shown me to was at the end of the passage, past the larger wards, only one other bed in it, and the low February sun pouring in. "It's lovely." I hesitated, turned back to her. "But there's been a mistake."

"No mistake," she said.

"I've only got third-class medical insurance."

"We know. But it's a major operation, and we'd like you to have this bed."

So cancer had its advantages!

After the student doctor and houseman had examined me and asked four sheetfuls of questions, I came back to the ward and put on one of the long summer dresses I'd brought as nightgown-substitutes. At home I slept naked, and all you could buy in Amsterdam shops, I discovered, were pajamas, which I didn't like wearing, or nightgowns, which were either wisps of nothingness made to be stripped off or thick ones printed with teddy bears apparently designed with ten-year-olds in mind. Two nightgowns were acceptable, but they didn't open down the front. These summer dresses had buttons all the way down. Oh, I can be practical when I choose.

The other woman in the room was on a chair now, talking into the phone.

She looked across at me as she put it down. "Hello. That was my husband. He wanted to know which vegetables to get for René and Alis. René's only four and he's a bit fussy about his food. Alis—she's the older one—she's OK. She helps me. I told him, ask Alis to help you, I said, but he won't listen. He doesn't like anyone else in the kitchen when he's cooking, says it breaks his concentration, and then he leaves all the pans dirty; but as I said to him last week, Rikki, I said, if you just wash them as you go along, it'd make life easier, or you could let me come in and wash them. And do you know what he said?"

I shook my head.

"Men are like that. He said men always make more mess so there's no point in me trying to change him. He read it in one of my magazines, he said. Men! What are you in for?"

"Mastectomy."

"Cancer then, is it?"

"Yes."

She pulled a face. "My sister had one of those three years back. They did it here. Every day I came in to see her. In this same wing, too. I never thought I'd end up here myself. Not that I'm in for the same thing, mind. Her mastectomy didn't do her any good. She's on her way out."

Ah. "So where did it spread to?" I was cold-blooded about finding out details of cancer. I'd read all the books I could find and those that publishing friends and colleagues had sent, staying up all night, buoyed up, insatiable.

"Her bones." She bit into an apple and chomped briskly. "She was in a bad way. I go home tomorrow. Are you afraid?"

I thought about it. "Not really." Or was I? In a funny way I'd suspended fear, hurtling along in the fast track where I'd been shunted by the system. Even at the beginning: various friends had told me that the waiting to see the surgeon was the worst time, but they'd been wrong. It had felt as if I was drifting, safe, in a cocoon, unreal.

"I'm Jan, by the way."

"Anya. Pleased to meet you."

"Why are you here?" I asked.

"Trouble with my plumbing. Not cancer though. I'm spared that, thank God. They told me that at the beginning: 'It's not cancer,' they said."

Right. I smiled. It was weirdly easier to cope with this bluntness. Gluey pity was worse. Or being told I'd be fine. Or being told I wasn't to talk about death—as one person, but only one, had said.

"I go home tomorrow. You'll have another roommate. Mind, they thought they'd caught my sister's in time. How about yours?"

I shrugged. "I'm not sure."

"How come?"

"I was diagnosed late. My own fault really." We both fell silent.

You never expect to get pregnant when you're very young, or catch a venereal disease: "It won't happen to me," you think. Same thing applied in a way to cancer, which is why I hadn't bothered much.

It wasn't even that I'd been unaware of it. In my late twenties in London, I'd gone to the doctor because of lumps in my breasts. "They're normal," he said, palpating them. "Some women just have lumpy breasts." In my early forties in Amsterdam, I'd worried again about lumps and had gone to the doctor I was then registered with. He sent me for a mammogram. "You're clear," they told me, "no need to worry." So I didn't. I even missed the lumpiness when the menopause a couple of years later smoothed out my breasts. So when, five years after that, I got lumpy breasts again, I welcomed them as old friends—and did nothing. My right breast did seem lumpier than the left, and admittedly that made me wonder, but I went along for the national screening when I turned fifty; if there was anything wrong, it would show up now. I said nothing. I heard nothing. I felt fine. I did nothing.

One year passed. The lumps seemed to be growing, or was I imagining it? My nipples rarely came out to play anymore. And in the night I felt a gnawing in my right breast; it became uncomfortable to lie on that side. "No one gets breast cancer in both breasts at once," said my doctor's assistant when I went for a routine smear and raised the matter. Again, I let it ride. Months later, I spotted a dent in the side of my right breast. I was too busy to do anything about it. Weeks later, feeling well, but with an obstinate case of thrush, I finally went to my GP. I'd broached it as an "Oh-by-the-way" when I was dressed again.

TEA CAME ROUND on the trolley, and Dr. Huizinga ambled in behind. "Fancy a talk?" He helped himself to a cup of tea and was already walking out of the room again, so I followed. In the side room, the surgeon perched on the table. "All right so far?"

"Fine. I'm lucky with the room, aren't I?"

He smiled. "We aim to please."

"What about a liver scan and a bone scan?" I asked. "When do I have those?" They hadn't been mentioned at my examination earlier, but according to the books I'd read, this was part of the process.

He shrugged. "There's no need. Time enough for those if you feel ill afterward."

I thought about the subtext. "And since if it's gone to my liver or bones, I don't want chemotherapy, there's no point, you mean?" We'd talked at length already about life, death, and the universe.

"Well, that is your standpoint. You said you wanted to get on with living." He paused.

"I do," I agreed.

"Once you come round from the operation, the clock will start ticking again."

I loved him for being such an optimist, so unalarming. The other doctors seemed more somber. I could have hugged my GP for getting me this surgeon.

"Tell me about you," he said. "Your work, your Simon."

I told him. I talked about translating for Radio Netherlands, in shifts that sometimes took up the night, a welcome change of pace though from the manuscripts that publishers sent me to translate. I told him about my aging, peripatetic parents and about Simon, my ex. And he talked about his new grandchild and his roses.

Simon came in later. We played backgammon. Simon had a glass of the vintage port Peter and Connie had given me when I'd gone down to stay the night in the country with them. We'd gone walking and Simon had joined us. I couldn't drink or eat because of the operation. I was second on the list for the morning.

THE FIRST THING I'd done when I came round from the operation was shout for painkillers. The injection came swiftly.

The first thing I did when I came round the second time was check that my left breast was still there. Before the operation, in the room where they wheel you in and leave you, comforted by the hot blankets a nurse had padded round me, two young doctors had approached with a clipboard. "Lumpectomy and mastectomy," one had said to the other across my relaxed body.

"Which side?"

"Right lumpectomy, left mastectomy."

I was startled, despite my drowsiness from the pre-med. "No, right mastectomy, left lumpectomy," I contradicted them.

They paused, a tube suspended in the air above me. They looked down. "Are you sure?"

"Of course." I nodded in slow motion.

"Oh, righto," said the first. "Tube into the left hand then, not the right."

. . .

Be absolute for death;
either death or life
shall thereby be the sweeter.
WILLIAM SHAKESPEARE,
Measure for Measure

Day two. Gray sky again, gradually lightening. I shifted onto my left side while the nurse took my temperature. I could only lie on my back and a bit on the left, what with the drain and my right arm being propped up on a pillow to help it drain and ease the soreness of the wound.

"You're doing ok." The nurse touched my cheek and left. "You can wash yourself today."

I slid out of bed, picked up the bottle attached to the drain, and shuffled off to one of the three wash cubicles for the whole wing of forty beds. No one else was up. The silent roommate who'd been wheeled in the night before wasn't stirring. It wasn't easy, strip-washing with a drain and an arm that hurt and couldn't be much maneuvered. And the chest area defeated me, I didn't touch it; but at last I was done and felt fresher. Back in the ward, I smoothed cream into my drying skin where I could, then got back into bed, exhausted. I watched the sky grow lighter and sang to myself in my head, the gloomiest hymns I could dredge up. They cheered me.

I waggled the fingers of my right hand where they rested on the pillow. I wondered.

I sat up and reached for my pen. Then for a postcard. I swung the table round over the bed.

I began to write! I wrote three postcards: to my parents, to Connie and Peter, to Hannah. My arm got no sorer than it was already. I began to shake and blub. I laid down the pen. I didn't want to tempt fate.

By the time the white coats came to surround my bed and stare at me, I was smiling again. Up and down like a yo-yo.

"It's rare to see someone so lively after an operation, especially one like this," said the ward surgeon.

The minute they'd gone, I felt blubby again, blubby and tired. "An operation like this," he'd said. Had I missed something? Was it even worse than I'd thought? My emotions tumbled and spun. I hated the pain where I had had a breast, but at least that would ease. I hated the numbness at the top of my arm more. It was part of me, but it wasn't my own body now. I was prodding it, trying to get sensation, any sensation, when Dr. Huizinga sauntered in, coat unbuttoned and flapping, as usual.

"How long will it stay numb?" I asked.

He smiled. "Good morning."

"Good morning." I stopped scowling.

He pulled up a chair. "It'll always be a bit numb," he said. "It's because the nerves are gone. But the numbness will diminish."

"Oh. And will it really be six months before I can get back to work? I can't spare six months!"

"Six months? Where did you hear that?"

"An editor. I got a letter yesterday saying it took her six months to get back to work, and then it was only part-time. I think she was trying to be comforting but . . . " I swallowed. "I'm freelance, she isn't. She can afford not to go to work. Anyway, I like my work."

"Throw away the letter," he said. "You're an optimist. You can go back to work when you're out of here, just a couple of days later. Rest when you feel tired, and you'll be fine. Some people need illness because it tells them who they are, but then they can't live life. You've had a dreadful operation, and it isn't easy, but you'll manage. Have you tried writing yet?"

I picked up one of the postcards and waved it triumphantly at him.

"There now. What did I tell you? All my patients have been able to use their arms afterward. You'll get used to the numbness; it's not important."

"Can I have baths?" I asked. I'd gathered a sheaf of leaflets about cancer on one of my sorties down the corridor and had got through half of them. The leaflet on lymphedema I'd braced myself for had warned against lying in hot baths, against shaving, against lifting, against getting knocked, against most things, as far as I could see.

"Of course you can lie in the bath. Do what you want; you're the best judge. If it feels wrong at first, stop it and try again later."

After he went, I wrote more cards, I read a chapter of *The Brothers Karamazov*, I chatted with the cleaner, I ate the food I'd chosen for lunch, I practiced lifting my arm above the blanket five times as the physiotherapist had instructed, and then turned on my tiny radio, put in earphones, and lay back, eyes closed, listening to Radio 4, dozing.

My new roommate, Erna: slight, Surinamese, eighty years old, as she told me with some pride. She looked only my age.

Her husband and son came for one hour every afternoon and sat silent at her bedside in helpless misery. She lay stretched before them, a medieval queen on her tomb.

"Why are you here?" I asked her on her second day, when I noticed her watching me.

"A lump," she said. "Here." She jabbed at her abdomen. "It's not a tumor," she added fiercely and shut her eyes again.

Oh right. What was it with me and my roommates and cancer?

She opened her eyes again. "What about you?" she asked with some effort, waving vaguely at my drains.

"Cancer," I said. "Four tumors. Breasts."

She looked horrified, and I was sorry I'd been so blunt.

"Sorry," she said, "I didn't mean it."

I smiled back to reassure her, but it was some time before she seemed to want to talk again. Then it was to ask about my accent.

"It's English," I told her.

"Ah." She nodded knowingly. "I've been there, to England. Once. It's an island, isn't it?"

Well, yes, and I went back often. I had always dreaded the idea of being in hospital in the Netherlands. When the chips are down, you'd want to be speaking your own language, wouldn't you? But events had overcome me, I'd been fast-tracked, and it had felt fine, and even after the operation when I'd screamed out for relief from pain, I had been surprised to hear myself scream in Dutch.

Erna, like me, wanted no television and no telephone. Ours was a peaceful ward. The nurses came to us to write up their notes and sit quietly at the table at the window and rest.

I liked fresh air and kept the window propped open with a magazine from a common room down the passage. Erna liked it too, never once complaining of the draft.

Fortunately. One night she broke through her constipation in the small hours, on a wheeled commode beside her bed. I was glad: she'd been uncomfortable and complaining.

I was less glad as daylight came and the commode was not removed, let alone emptied. I looked for a nurse. Sunday morning and I could find only one, five wards away, and she had her hands full.

I opened the window as wide as the rolled-up magazine would allow. I shook drops of lavender oil into the air, but still the room stank, and still the commode stood there. Erna herself seemed comatose. Embarrassed, I suspected.

Breakfast arrived.

I looked again for a nurse and this time made a fuss. At last two came, seconded from downstairs, they told me, and cleared the commode away. Erna smiled tentatively at me and I nodded happily, my mouth full of bread and honey.

After breakfast, volunteers came for me as requested, with a wheelchair: two strangers. They hid the bottle and drain in folds of blankets, "We don't want to see those, do we?" and pushed me to the chapel. There we were, a bunch of cripples and maimed, the dying and the hopeful, in wheelchairs and hospital beds. The singing was uncertain and ragged, punctuated by coughs and sighs, but the priest was young and sincere.

All I wanted after the mass was silence.

They wheeled me back, two of them, cheerful and chattering at and over me; it was rather like being at the hairdresser. You have to watch the cheerful, the well meaning. What you want is the low key, the blunt, the normal, those like the Turkish ward orderly in her headscarf and sweet smile who had stopped her brushing the morning of my operation to ask, "Aren't you scared? I would be." Then I could open and talk. Avoid the brightly cheerful if you can.

I got out of the chair at the entrance to my wing and walked the last stretch. I wanted to be alone. A small furry head lay on my pillow. While I'd been away, the nurses had made up the bed and tucked in Tom Bear. His dark woolen eyes looked up at me. I got in and cuddled him.

Later that morning, lying quietly, I farted.

There was a mutter from the prone figure on the other bed. Erna raised herself an inch or two, pointed a bony finger at me. "You farted!" she cackled, "I heard you: tee, hee, hee!

"In Suriname," she went on, "we say farting will kill you."

"Really?"

"Mmm." She was almost sitting up now in her excitement. "It's because of a nineteenth-century tombstone over the border in Guyana. Everyone knows about it. It goes . . . " and she declaimed in English:

Fart free, wherever you may be
for farting is the death of me.

"You see? You'll die of it. Tee, hee, hee."

That afternoon I had a crowd of visitors: Simon with two thermoses of mint tea, Hannah with yet another bottle of champagne, and several from church—Katherine and Joshua, and Helen and her ten-year-old daughter, Judith—even my GP. Simon poured the champagne. I took a sip or two, it was all I could manage, then I told them the farting story, to the accompaniment of cackles from the other bed. Judith jumped to her feet and broke out into familiar hymn music:

Fart free, wherever you may be.

and we joined in noisily, an evangelical scratch choir:

I am the lord of the fart, said he . . .

"Tee hee hee," shrieked Erna from her bed.

A man hath no better thing under the sun, than
to eat, and to drink, and to be merry: for that shall
abide with him of his labour the days of his life,
which God giveth him under the sun.

ECCLESIASTES

A doctor appeared at my side. I turned my head and smiled, recognizing him. It was the young houseman who'd examined me the day I'd arrived, the day before the operation, before I'd been mutilated, when I was still whole. He'd been pretty silent then. I could imagine nurses falling for that and his cornily attractive deep blue eyes and messy hair.

"Nice position you've got here." He nodded out at the window and the sun. He tweaked my curtain a bit to shield me as a ray streaked through to hit my bed. "It must get hot sometimes in the middle of the day."

I shook my head. "I like it."

He didn't take the hint and pull the curtain back. "How are you feeling today? How's the arm?"

I lifted it the prescribed six inches off the pillow before wincing. "It's OK. Look. And I've been writing a bit."

"Good."

I was pleased to have his approval. "The wound's OK too."

"Good. Good. Of course, you realize . . . " he paused, then went on. "You do realize that a couple of the lymph glands were affected."

It was a statement, not a question. The blood drained from my face. It had never occurred to me that they might be. I'd assumed they were taken out as a preventive measure. I'd never thought to ask, I'd been concentrating solely on my breasts. Stupid, stupid!

"Not to worry though."

"Oh. No. Right."

"Good. See you." He was gone with a swish of the white coat.

I lie. It wasn't like that.

"Does that mean the cancer's more likely to have spread?" was what I asked.

"More likely, yes, but it may not have done."

Silence, for which I was grateful.

"It's all right, though, really," I said, thinking aloud. "I've had a great life, and if this does mean death, it's fine, I can accept it."

"That's not the common attitude." He relaxed, visibly.

"We can't all live into our eighties and nineties. Why should I?" I was fine as long as I was talking. "If you had cancer," I asked him, "would you grab everything on offer, go for trials, that sort of thing? Or would you accept death coming—if it was advanced, I mean."

"Is this something I have to answer?"

I nodded.

"I wouldn't take treatment at any price, no," he said.

"So you're not afraid of dying yourself?"

He laughed. "Patients don't usually ask me that."

"Are you?"

"Since you ask. I don't think I am, no." He fiddled with his stethoscope. "I must get on. You'll be OK?"

I nodded.

That was true until he'd left the room. Then I felt desperately sorry for myself. Such a weird disease, creeping through your body without your noticing. First you have lumps, but you feel fine. You're whisked into hospital and they mutilate you, and suddenly you're not fine at all. A tear trickled out of my eye, followed by another and another. I blinked them back. I turned toward the window and let them fall; I wasn't able to stop them.

But tears don't change anything. I blew my nose hard. I picked up Marcus Aurelius's *Meditations*, opened it at random, and read through watering eyes: "Whatsoever is, is but the seed of that which shall be." Thanks a lot, I said silently, and put the book down smartly.

It mightn't matter, I reassured myself. You don't feel any worse than you did before, and that wasn't ill at all. I'd just ignored lumps, for too long. And now I was scared, and yet not scared.

I slid out of bed, picked up my drain bottle, and went down the corridor, looking for a phone.

A tall, slim woman was coming toward me. "Hannah! What are you doing here?"

"Coming to see you." She turned me round and, seeing my watery eyes, left her arm round my shoulders. "I had a meeting down the road and thought I'd see if I could come up."

"And they didn't stop you?"

"As you see."

I got back into bed and she sat on the end. She peeled me a clementine and handed it over, then peeled one for herself.

"What's up?" she asked, and it all came pouring out.

She told me about a Trappist monastery where she'd been on retreat on the weekend, meditating, while Sophie was with her father. "Could that be something for you?" she suggested.

Maybe. I took down the number of the monastery. It would be something to try. I'd often wanted to go on retreat, but hadn't known where or how to go about it.

The lunch trolley turned up, rubber wheels squeaking. "I'll be off." She got down from the bed and we kissed.

Earth to earth, ashes to ashes, dust to dust.

THE BOOK OF COMMON PRAYER

I'd always imagined that the Jewish custom of sitting shivah for seven days and reciting the Kaddish would be about death and mourning. It isn't. At least, not directly. The Kaddish is all about how great God is, and the newly bereaved are greeted with: "I wish you long life." Death is part of life, and life goes on regardless. Oddly comforting. Like the classic passage from *Ecclesiastes* that I'd like read at my funeral:

> To every thing there is a season, and a time to every
> purpose under the heaven:

A time to be born, and a time to die; a time to plant
and a time to pluck up that which is planted;
A time to kill, and a time to heal; a time to break
down, and a time to build up;
A time to weep, and a time to laugh; a time to
mourn, and a time to dance . . .
I have seen the travail which God hath given to the
sons of men to be exercised in it.
He hath made every thing beautiful in his time; also
he hath set the world in their heart, so that no
man can find out the work that God maketh
from the beginning to the end.
I know that there is no good in them, but for a man
to rejoice, and to do good in his life.
And also that every man should eat and drink, and
enjoy the good of all his labour, it is the gift of
God.
I know that, whatsoever God doeth, it shall be for
ever: nothing can be put to it, nor any thing
taken from it: and God doeth it, that men
should fear before him.
That which hath been is now; and that which is to
be hath already been; and God requireth that
which is past.

I was glad I was religious, glad that there was a ritual ready and waiting. What would be wonderful was if four friends carried the coffin into church, not the funereal crows from the undertaker's. I'd like to wait at home in my coffin and for friends to come round and drink and eat and talk over me. Then be cycled to church on a bicycle cart. A service in church, not in some bland crematorium space, sanitized against religion. A service with this passage and later maybe the famous one from St. Paul's Letter to the Corinthians about love: "For now we see through a glass, darkly; but then face to face: now I know in part; but then shall I know even as also I am known." At the end, Boëllmann's glorious "Toccata" on the organ.

I spent a long time thinking about the hymns. Should I go for my favorites, whatever they were? Or for what was suitable? I liked "Abide with me," but it had become corny, and I didn't want manipulated blubbing. Or should I go for strong, positive ones? One would be "Guide me, O thou great Jehovah," I decided: at least friends who didn't go to church but watched sport on television would be likely to know that, no matter what their nationality. I lay there, singing hymns in my mind, eliminating some, choosing others, none too obscure or difficult. Once that was settled, I moved on to the burial.

Despite all these years living away, what I really wanted was to be buried in England, to rot into the English soil in a country churchyard, there for eternity, unlike here where they dig you up after God knows how few years. On the other hand, with no children, no husband, who would come to put flowers on my grave? And there was the impracticality of the journey. That left Zorgvlied Graveyard along the river. Or maybe, better, the Eastern Graveyard: sunnier and more open. I'd go into the earth, there to rot. I wanted that rotting, my flesh disintegrating into worms and soil. Let it be said as it is. Earth to earth. For that reason, the coffin could even be thick cardboard: cheap and temporary. The money would be better spent on a party afterward, not there at the graveyard. A party with lots of booze and food and music, where people could get up on their hind legs and spout if they really felt it necessary, and otherwise be as cheerful or trivial or maudlin as they cared as life took over again.

I wished I could be there. I would be, of course, though they wouldn't see me. Ghost at my own funeral. Pity to miss the wine.

All things that are in the world are always in the estate of alteration. Thou also art in a perpetual change, yea and under corruption too, in some part: and so is the whole world.

MARCUS AURELIUS, *Meditations*

"These are the most realistic, of course."

The woman from the Breast Cancer Association opened a box. Inside nestled a transparent blob.

"Take it out," she encouraged me.

I lifted the blob. It was cold. I put it on the table. It quivered, reminding me of Victorian aspic jelly, or a jellyfish with armature.

"Thanks." I put it back in the box, closed the lid, and slid it back across the table to her. We were alone, in the side room, I in my dress and dressing gown, she in full makeup.

"You would get used to it," she said, with a brassy, well-groomed smile.

"I might," I agreed, "but I still wouldn't like it."

Determined not to be thwarted, she pushed leaflets at me. "Ring us when you've thought about it. I've been wearing them for, oh, ten years now. No one notices the difference."

I looked at her. I dare say they didn't. But breasts are for suckling and for sex. Why pretend, why bother with false blobs? Imagine stripping off for a lover, I thought. It would be worse even than wondering at what moment to take off your mascara.

"You don't have to see her if you don't want to," the young nurse had told me. But I'd gone happily, not expecting it to be a problem.

"Take this anyway as a stopgap," the woman said. In her hand was a sponge inset, not unlike a shoulder pad. "You'll need a safety pin to fix it to the cup of your bra," she said.

I hadn't worn a bra since my twenties.

"The only snag is that the bra tends to ride round your body—that's why we recommend these; they're heavier." She tapped the yellow box. "Well, then. Back to the ward," she said, all jollity still. "You mustn't worry, you know. I had my mastectomy eleven years ago, and look at me now."

I looked at her face, set in lines of relentless good cheer, relieved that our session was over. Didn't she realize that I wasn't bothered about survival? All I wanted to cope with was now.

*Let it be thy perpetual meditation, how
many physicians who once looked so grim, and
so theatrically shrunk their brows upon their
patients, are dead and gone themselves.*

MARCUS AURELIUS, *Meditations*

"We have to speak to you." This was the controlling nurse, the only one I didn't like much, even if her daily anti-thrombosis injections were featherlight.

"Oh. Speak," I said.

"But you have someone with you." She gestured at Jules, the minister from the church where I went in the Begijnhof, Helen's husband, who had come to see me; as a clergyman, he didn't have to keep to visiting hours.

"That's all right," I said.

She smiled tightly and flicked at my sheet. "It's for the results of your biopsy."

"Fine. I don't mind Jules hearing. You don't either, do you?" I asked him, just in case.

"Not at all."

She didn't look all that happy.

"So what was it you wanted to say? What are the results?"

"Not here," she said. "Come through to the side room."

Oh help. That changed things. It could only mean trouble. My mouth dried. She laid a hand on my arm as I swung my legs out of bed. "Now you mustn't worry."

I started worrying.

We followed her. "Why don't you sit there," she said, pointing to two empty chairs. Near them was the student doctor. "Hello." I was glad to see her. She'd been several times to my bed, just to talk. The smile I got back looked tense.

Jules sat to my side. Arranged in a semicircle facing us were four others, seated. It was like going for an interview, except that I didn't know what I was applying for. From the grave expressions on their faces it looked as if I'd lost the job anyway.

One young man opposite cleared his throat. His hair was so blond it might not have existed, and his cheeks looked in bad need of wind and winter sun. Was he one of the gaggle of doctors that stood around my bed every morning? I wasn't sure. The other three introduced themselves in turn, but their names meant nothing to me.

"We've had the results of your biopsy," the blond doctor said, leaning forward as if to say, Trust me.

My stomach clenched.

"As you know, we removed sixteen of your lymph glands along with the breast."

I nodded. Here it comes. Wait for it.

"Two were malignant. Cancerous," he added, in case I didn't know the meaning of the word.

"Oh? What else?" I said, in tight control of myself, prepared to hear the worst.

"What *else*? Nothing else."

"I thought you were going to tell me something dreadful." I was beaming in relief.

"Well, it's not nothing," the nurse began. "Do you understand what the doctor has just told you?"

"Yes." I made myself look serious again for their benefit. "Only, I knew that already," I added.

"How?" the doctor asked.

"Your colleague told me. Days ago."

"Really? Which one?"

"Dark hair, blue eyes. I'm sorry, I'm hopeless at names. I was grateful to him for telling me."

"He shouldn't have done." A flush crept across the doctor's pallor.

I shrugged.

The semicircled white coats looked at each other.

"Look it up on the Internet, ask us anything you like," the doctor said at last. "The affected glands were nearer your armpit than your neck, which is better than it could be. Have you got any questions?"

I couldn't think of any. "Is that it? May I go?"

They looked nonplussed. The student seemed to be holding in laughter. "Yes," the blond doctor said.

Jules and I left the room. "Did I miss something?" I asked. "What was all that about?"

He was grinning. "It's policy nowadays to break bad news that way. They call it the 'Bad News Talk.' You weren't supposed to have been told already. The idea is that the nurse who brought you in should be there for you afterward, to pick up the pieces."

"There aren't any pieces," I said, "unless I did indeed miss something. There wasn't anything new in there, was there?"

He shrugged. "You tell me. I don't think so."

I'd rung him weepily after that first time I'd been told, after Hannah had left, and he'd come straight round to see me. As he had the day before I'd gone into hospital when I'd had a bout of panic and despair and Simon had been out of town.

"Have a glass of port with me," I said, in case I reacted after all.

But I didn't. He drank his glass of port and most of mine too, and left. I wondered if there was something wrong with my reactions.

When he was gone, I felt weary. The sky was lowering. Rain began beating on the glass. The roofs were disappearing in gray-yellow cloud and lights were coming on. I turned on my side and slept.

· · ·

There is no man that hath power
over the spirit to retain the spirit; neither
hath he power in the day of death.

ECCLESIASTES

Hospital had been simple. Go in, be cut open, recover and, ten days later, get out.

Afterward was more complicated. I liked being alone usually, but not now. Besides, I was pathetically weak and weary. Now I needed people around me. I went to the country to Peter and Connie's the first weekend. It was there that I had my first shower since the operation.

You hear about animals who try to eat away a limb that is damaged and hanging numb and useless. Marie had given me tea-tree shower gel. I'd never used shower gel before, preferring soap. But I did now: flannel and soap would be too rough. Besides, the only way to reclaim the numb parts of me and the scooped-out chest was with my hands.

It was horrible. This is numb, and this and this. Saying it out aloud to myself helped. It hurts, I sobbed out, smoothing over the fresh scar, forcing my soapy, slippery hands over my body. I shall get used to it. This hurts, all this. It will get better. My face was as wet with tears as with shower water by the time I turned it off. I wrapped myself in a huge bath towel and carefully patted myself dry. It was just me, getting used to the new me. I stared long and coolly in the mirror, splashed my eyes with cold water. "Hello," I said to me. Tomorrow, I promised myself, I'd try having a bath.

Once my face was back to a normal color, I joined them at the fireside for drinks.

Two days later, back in town, I went cheerfully to my GP for the stitches to be taken out.

I screamed.

Nobody had told me this would hurt. He persevered. I wept. His hand shook. He chucked pills and pessaries at me: "Take these," he said, and stepped back from the couch, shaking, looking drained, "and come back in two hours."

Two hours later it was fine. I sat rather than lay on the couch, and the painkillers and tranquilizers had done their job. I didn't understand it though; it shouldn't have been painful, not psychologically, at any rate. I had had no fear of the stitches coming out. Ma, clever Ma, rang that night to check up on me. "I knew it might hurt," she said.

*Our critical day is not the very day of
our death; but the whole course of our life.*

JOHN DONNE

There's a thing called the Cancer Committee. Eight good men and true: surgeons, oncologists, radiologists, hematologists, Lord knows who else. Dr. Huizinga was part of the Committee, and I had an appointment to see him a week after leaving hospital, to see what course of treatment they had decided upon. Simon and I went there from a café where I'd insisted on filling him in on cancer treatments, using him as a sounding board. I said that if chemotherapy was offered, I thought I would refuse it. I didn't want to be made to feel ill on top of feeling so tired now the operation was over. I wanted to get better, get on with living. I might refuse the radiotherapy too, I said, even though a first appointment had already been made. Simon didn't argue.

But I was nervous going into the consulting room.

"I've canceled the radiotherapy for you."

I could have kissed Dr. Huizinga.

"I had to argue with most of them; the oncologist and the radiologist took some persuading." He pulled a piece of paper toward him and sketched the site of a breast. "Here and here and here were your tumors." Three crosses. "This is where they're currently giving radiotherapy to mastectomy patients," he drew a vertical line, "down the breastbone. There's a good reason for that: my knife can't get underneath there for tumors. But . . ." his pen moved again, "the shoots from your tumors went sideways to your armpit, not the other way to the breastbone. This radiotherapy is the standard protocol; call it treatment for statistics' sake if you're feeling skeptical, trial and error if not. Since you made your views clear on the subject . . ."

"You canceled it." I was elated. "Thank you. But what about the appointment I've got for it, on Monday?"

"We'll take care of that."

"I don't have to ring? Really?"

"No." He raised a hand, "Wait. I haven't finished."

I subsided. "You're not going to say chemotherapy now, are you?"

"No," he smiled. "Tamoxifen." The usual treatment for postmenopausal women. A pill a day, estrogen-blocking. I knew about that, more or less. "For five years."

"Why five?" asked Simon.

He licked his finger, stuck it in the air and shrugged. "It used to be two years, now it's five. Who knows?"

"Right." I pushed back my chair and was about to get up.

"And . . . " he stopped me. "There'll be a mammogram every year and I'll want to see you at the same time. We need to keep an eye on the other breast."

"Fine," and it was. It was good to know that I'd be seeing him again. I hoped that if it ever spread, he'd still be around. I hoped he wouldn't have retired, and didn't want to know his age, in case. "We're going for a drink to celebrate," Simon said as soon as we were out on the street again. From that café we went to another. We talked about living and dying. We drank quite a lot. One thing led to another and we ended up in bed together and he touched me gently and we made love and I felt whole. It was a gift from a friend, no more, no less.

If thou shalt look backward: behold, what an
infinite chaos of time doth present itself unto thee;
and as infinite a chaos, if thou shalt look forward.
In that which is so infinite, what difference can
there be between that which liveth but three days,
and that which liveth three ages?
MARCUS AURELIUS, *Meditations*

I t had always been intriguing lying in
bed in the mornings, snug, trying not
to get up, unraveling the dreams of the night and wondering
at their obscure meanings. Now it was different, no fun. All
dreams were nightmares. They lacked subtlety and ambiguity. The most brutally direct one recurred.

I was in the coupling between two railway carriages; the
floor slid and shifted beneath me. The train was hurtling
forward at high speed, shaking me. A cold wind blasted at
me. I was unable to move. I opened my eyes and saw that I
was surrounded by people. Their faces were leaning over

me. As soon as they saw that I was looking, they reached down as one and clawed at my breast. They tore shreds and lumps from it, leering at me and laughing. And all the while the train raced on. No one came to my aid.

I woke in pain. I went downstairs to shake off the horror, made myself a hot-water bottle and chamomile tea and took them back to bed, lit the candle at the side of the bed, and read poetry till I was soothed and my eyelids drooped once more.

Over the months the nightmares eased, giving way to restless nights during which I replayed scene after scene. At first it was like prying the scab off a healing wound, but the more I scratched, the less awful it became. With each replay, the horror diminished. Days were never a problem: work was too much of a distraction. I made no plans. I changed nothing. Why should I? I was content, if weary. I rested for half an hour every day for awhile but was back at work translating within less than a week, and back at the radio—though no night shifts at first—within three weeks.

I gave myself treats too, one a day. Small ones, such as taking whatever translation was on the go to a café and working on it there over a long cup of coffee, instead of in my office at home. And walking there rather than quickly cycling, partly for the pleasure of it, partly to build up my strength.

I was lucky to have friends. You need them, and yet it's friends, and talking, that are tiring. I needed silence too; I wanted to hibernate and daydream, absorb, mend—but within the context of their friendship. I saw Simon, Marie, Hannah, Connie, and Peter the most. They were all kind and generous to me, even when I was too tired to talk. Telephone calls from them and others, asking how I was, were the most exhausting. I wanted to be left alone. I was glad to see them and hear them. Such ambivalence. That too got better as I became less tired.

One day over coffee in the café where I was working, Simon told me about Alex. He'd met her in Turkey, wandering round a ruin. It probably didn't mean anything, he added.

An editor in publishing who sometimes gave me proposals to translate, not someone I was especially close to, had a lumpectomy. She, like me, was pleased with how it went. She, like me, had a couple of lymph glands affected. She rang and asked if I'd like to have a drink.

"It's so irresponsible of people not to have radiotherapy," she sputtered over her wine. She wasn't a tactless woman, only forthright, so I reckoned she'd forgotten that I hadn't. She was seeing a psychologist, she told me, once a week for counseling. I gathered that I would have been offered that if

I'd gone for radiotherapy and, with it, the three-monthly checkups. For this, too, she was grateful. But I didn't regret the lack. Other people went to counselors. I went to church. Quite apart from God and worship and faith, I like the way it puts me into perspective, makes my health relative.

The first Sunday I was back in church, my arm still in a sling to ease the pain, people responded warmly. Far from avoiding me, they came over. Most touched me, on the arm, the cheek, tentatively, as if they were superstitiously touching wood.

The biddies were not so tentative. At the end of the service they came over and hugged me. It was useless to brandish the sling since they knew my arm wasn't broken. It was useless trying to hold them off. They didn't notice. They thought my tears were of emotion not of pain, for which you couldn't blame them since I was smiling through the tears at their warmth. I retreated step by step to the safety of a corner so that they could no longer clutch me to them.

There is no remembrance of former things, neither shall there be any remembrance of things that are to come with those that shall come after.

ECCLESIASTES

The monastery near the Belgian border, which Hannah had recommended, helped recovery. Four days of not talking, four days of meditation interspersed with singing in chapel with the monks, four days of intensity and rest. There was a constant play between the visible, audible, and tangible, and the invisible, inaudible, and intangible, between earth and heaven. It was all that mattered. I was cut off from society, and yet was wholly present. At first, my head felt leaden as anxieties surfaced and accumulated, and it ached on my shoulders as I sat cross-legged trying to meditate, trying to empty my mind. That eased.

I got to know my fellow guests on retreat not from their

voice or accent or profession but by what they ate at breakfast (which cheese, which spread, which combination, whether tea, coffee, or fresh milk from the monks' own cows) and whether, as most Dutch do, they used a knife and fork to eat their bread and jam. I noticed who looked tired, who unhappy, who tense, who calm, who centered, and how some changed over the days, as I did. In chapel, I heard who sang sweetly, who shyly, who not at all. At the first meditation, as daylight began to fill the room, the silence was deep and intense. At the final meditation of the day, the room dimmed again and those across from me with their backs to the window took on the silhouette of a row of buddhas against the gathering gloom. As, still in silence, we scattered outside under the trees to drink a last cup of herb tea before night and summer chill drove us indoors, rabbits gamboled undisturbed on the grass. Lights out at ten. In bed, a phrase that we chanted unaccompanied in chapel sang round and round my head: "Lord, you have words of eternal life: whom else can we turn to?" as I dropped into a deep sleep.

I took the feeling with me when I left. I got up earlier, meditated in the mornings, and I fancied that it calmed me for the day.

AS THE WEEKS PASSED and I got stronger, I saw less of Simon, and thought little of it. Then one day he rang, to tell me he'd fallen in love.

The three of us met in a café. Simon flapped about as we maneuvered into position round the table, clearly anxious that Alex and I would get on, and ordered our drinks diffidently, wine for me, beer for him and her.

He'd told me she wore a surprising amount of makeup, but even so I was taken aback. She was our age, but completely different, superficially. She had a real hairdo, a perm even, she was carefully dressed, well groomed, and I suspected that she wouldn't dream of setting foot outside the door without her face on. She looked well heeled. All old-fashioned terms springing into my head, but they suited her. I felt as if I'd stepped back a generation.

But she was entertaining. At first we hedged about, trying to get comfortable with each other, but I soon relaxed, as did she, and it was then that I began to see what it was that appealed to him. Like him—and me—she'd traveled, she was quick with words, and they had a lively banter going; I soon gathered that she shared his love of games and quizzes and crosswords too. There was also an underlying earthiness beneath that polish, a depth to her laughter that I could imagine was sexy.

"We're going to Scotland on Tuesday for a week." Simon paused. "To fish."

He grinned to see the effect it had on me. I spluttered into my wine. "You never," I said. "Fishing?"

He waved at Alex who was smiling contentedly. "She goes coarse fishing," he said. "I shall sit on the bank and admire her."

"You mean,"—I turned to her—"standing in a river in waders with water up to your thighs (she was quite short) fishing for trout and the like?" It didn't fit at all.

"*And* she makes her own flies," Simon boasted.

"Wow." I was impressed. Delicate flies. Coarse fishing.

It wasn't difficult to like her, even though we were so unalike. And she clearly loved him, and he her, he was aglow.

Cycling home, I realized that with her delight in punning, her stature, her appearance, Alex had reminded me of someone: Simon's late mother.

SIX WEEKS LATER it was Christmas. I'd always made much of it and Simon had enjoyed that so I asked him if they'd both like to come round for the English-type Christmas dinner, homemade Christmas pud, the lot. They came. There was a small crowd of us and we played cards in a sozzled sort of way after dinner.

"You've got lots of photographs, Simon says," Alex turned to me, yawning, after we'd been playing for some time. "Of the last few years, I mean. I'd love to see them."

"Oh. Really?" I couldn't put my finger on why it seemed an odd request. "Are you sure?"

"Yes." She nodded, confident.

I fetched the albums and she took them over to the sofa as the rest of us went on playing. Every now and again I glanced over and noticed her methodically studying them.

She rejoined us. "I'd very much like to have the photographs of Simon," she said.

I couldn't have heard her properly. But her gaze was steady on me. I must have done. "Sorry," I said. "No. I don't want to break up the album." Then, as an afterthought, "If you like, you could pick out some and I'll have copies made."

She looked away. "Don't bother."

I thought no more of it then.

IN THE SPRING they moved in together. Or rather, Simon moved in with her, out of town, near the dunes and the sea.

As for the body, why should I make the
grief of my body to be the grief of my mind?
MARCUS AURELIUS, *Meditations*

Billy, a young Englishman who had once painted my patio walls, turned up at the door. He said he'd heard that I had cancer. I abandoned my translation and made us coffee.

He pulled a face. "Coffee isn't good for you."

"Only one cup a day, and that isn't even strong," I said.

"You need to cleanse your system."

"It's clean," I said firmly, getting irritated. Besides, Marie had read that research had shown that coffee mopped up the radicals and was therefore good, not bad, for cancer. And, conversely, a publisher had sent me a food book for breast-cancer patients, full of how good soya was for you, soya with this and soya with that. Two days later I read in the paper that soya was under investigation as being a suspect in encouraging malignant cell division.

I decided it was best to ignore all advice and eat as I always had, which was healthily anyway. I enjoy my food. I love crunchy grainy bread with the seeds that get stuck in your teeth, I love oily mackerel baked in the oven with herbs, rich organic butter from the farmers' market, goats' cheese, free-range eggs poached with the yolk sloshing over toast, the occasional beef or lamb dish stewed all day, slowly, in wine, and always loads of vegetables and ripe fruit till the juice comes out of my ears. I never eat processed or frozen foods, or tinned, except for sardines and Italian tomatoes in winter. My only additive is a disgusting teaspoonful of cod-liver oil every morning, washed swiftly down with a squeezed orange. I buy from markets, never supermarkets. You see? I'm choosy enough as it is. I don't want to get neurotic. Besides, I love chocolate cake, too, as a treat, in a café with coffee.

Despite being a builder, Billy was pale and skinny. He never touched butter because of the cholesterol and thought cream and meat the height of stupidity.

"I've brought you this." He passed a book across the table to me. "It'll help you," he said kindly.

It was about healing, aimed at the popular market, with lots of diagrams of chakras and suchlike.

"Positive thinking's very important," he told me eagerly, hair falling into his eyes. "This tells you how to heal yourself. No, don't ignore it," he said as I flicked through the pages and set it aside, having registered how simplistic it was.

Positive thinking! Heal yourself! Crass and facile. If you follow the argument through, it makes it your fault if the cancer spreads onward and, come to that, your fault even for getting it in the first place.

I do believe in the power of the mind. People do wait on their deathbed for a loved one; unhappiness can make you feel worse. And miracles do happen. But the mind isn't infallible; we can't control everything and we do have to die of something. We can't defeat every disease; something has to get us. Let life seep in and embrace it, but I doubt that you can think positively artificially. Enjoying life is more to the point, and it's either in your nature to be able to, or not. The rest is hogwash. I've no intention of being guilty of my own death.

The force that drew me away from life . . .
was a force like that of my previous attachment
to life, only in a contrary direction.

LEO TOLSTOY

At first I was just happy. Something horrid had been a good experience, thanks to those involved. It hurt and I looked lopsided, but how often do you get the chance to hear funeral eulogies before you die? To hear from friends how much they care about you? How can you possibly then be miserable? Cancer has its advantages. Anyway, I thought I'd be dead soon-ish, and that intensified every smell, sight, touch, taste, and sharpened every pleasure.

A year later it was different. It wasn't easy to adjust. You can't live at that peak forever, can you? But I missed the intensity. The problem isn't thinking you might die; it's think-ing you might live. Now that there was no sign of spread, dared I think "future" again? When friends said I looked well and was I? I didn't answer "yes," which was how I felt; I said "I hope so." Confusion and cancerchondria reigned.

Sometimes it was as if I wanted to know that I was dying so that I would know exactly where I stood and things could become simple and immediate once more. I'd get back that feeling of alive-ness. I felt ungrateful, ungra-cious. Oh, it wasn't that I seemed depressed or gloomy to the outside world; it was more a feeling that I was missing some spark. A sense of anticlimax, perhaps. That then made me worry that perhaps I was a drama queen. Might I survive beyond two years? Five? I wasn't even sure that I wanted to. I wished someone could tell me. I knew they couldn't. And I didn't like this new self-absorption and gloom that sometimes hit me.

I must have asked Dr. Huizinga everything under the sun about cancer. The one thing I had never asked was how he rated my chances. I didn't want to. He'd said nothing. I assume it's policy not to tell what isn't asked. Then I read in the science supplement of the Saturday paper that my par-ticular chances were sixty–forty, against. But, "There are lies, damned lies, and statistics." Dum-de-dum. And statis-tics are meaningless on a personal level. If you're in the forty percent, then you've got a one hundred percent chance of survival. Equally I could be one of the sixty percent, in which case I've got a one hundred percent chance of death within five years.

Anyway, as everyone constantly assured me, I might get run over by a tram. Accurate, but hardly relevant.

*The voice said, Cry. And he said, What shall I
cry? All flesh is grass, and all the goodliness thereof
is as the flower of the field: The grass withereth, the
flower fadeth: because the spirit of the Lord bloweth
upon it: surely the people is grass.*

ISAIAH

"You're so brave, Jan," they say, and I
shake my head. Just having cancer
doesn't turn you into a hero. Undergoing something you
can do nothing about isn't brave. Being as you are isn't
brave. I'm lucky: so far I accept it is as it is, and I'm coping
all right. Being brave is doing something against your nature. Coping isn't being brave, it's a gift.

Even so, I started turning up at my doctor's where pre-
cancer I wouldn't have. Pre-cancer, I'd been pretty much a
stranger at his surgery.

The first bit of cancerchondria was when an ache de-
veloped in my lower back and groin. Endometrial cancer, I

decided, the womb lining turning cancerous as a known, but rare, side effect of tamoxifen.

My doctor shook his head. "Unlikely," he said. "It's the bones I'm worried about," and he sent me back to hospital for another X ray.

If I'd had those three-monthly checkups at the specialist cancer hospital as in the protocol, like my colleague and everyone else, I could have mentioned these problems then and they could have been dismissed. Going to the doctor each time made it more of a big deal. I didn't want to cry wolf, yet nor should I ignore signs as I had before. Maybe aches and pains were just me getting older. They must have been: the X ray showed up nothing.

BUT WALKING TO my annual mammogram I feel brave. I walk briskly, but my feet are heavy. I want to run away. I tell no one I'm going, not even Simon, Marie, or Hannah. It is the same time of year I'd been diagnosed, January, cold, sunny—I'm convinced it'll recur in the other breast.

Back outside, cleared for another year, I don't believe the verdict. What about the pulling I feel inside my left breast and armpit, the weird spots round my mouth, the nails on my hand cracking and my toenails splitting, the dizziness, the slight weight loss, the mole that bled after a knock?

Oh, cancerchondria still hit all right. Fortunately, it hit less often. It was just tiredness and aging. No big deal. Two days later I'd forgotten all this. Two months later, few of those signs were there anyway.

Whatsoever is material, doth soon vanish away
into the common substance of the whole; and
whatsoever is formal, or whatsoever doth animate
that which is material, is soon resumed into the
common reason of the whole; and the fame and
memory of anything is soon swallowed up by the
general age and duration of the whole.
MARCUS AURELIUS, *Meditations*

"**H**ave you never considered breast reconstruction?"

I was at a translators' workshop and it was a Swedish publisher asking, a woman, the first ever to bring it up.

"What's the point? Breasts are for suckling and for sex," I trotted out. "I shan't be having a baby. I don't see a reconstructed breast helping during lovemaking."

"But to make you feel more . . . whole?" She was looking at my top.

"I'm not whole, so why pretend? Nor do I feel less of a woman." Mind you, I was wearing my hair longer than I had before the mastectomy. Was that to accentuate femininity?

It might be different of course if I were big-breasted. That must be uncomfortable: you'd be off-balance and it'd be bad for the spine. But I was smaller anyway than I had been because of the bite being chomped from my left breast (and weirder, since in the chomping, the nipple had traveled off-center, about half an inch toward my armpit).

I didn't think it was a problem for other people. If it was, they weren't saying.

They say that in the U.S., breast reconstruction is proposed before you go for the operation, as a matter of course. Thank God I don't live there. It's only natural to consider seriously what doctors offer, especially when you're feeling vulnerable; I was glad not to have had to consider that on top of the mastectomy. Choice is the mantra nowadays, but life can be so much more straightforward without it.

The previous October I'd been to the international book fair in Frankfurt, curious to see what it was like. I was striding past an Eastern European stand when suddenly a woman in her twenties came rushing out. She grabbed me in a big hug, kissed me warmly, and wept.

She thinks I'm someone else, I thought, startled.

"Thank you, oh, thank you," she sobbed.

When she finally drew away, I said, "What are you thanking me for? Who do you think I am?"

"Thank you for walking round like that," she said, pointing to my carved-out chest. "I've just lost my best friend to breast cancer, and she never dared to do anything like that, and I wish she had. From the moment she got cancer, she pretended, and the worst pretense was having a false breast. Thank you, thank you," smiling and sobbing.

"That's OK." I wasn't sure what else to say.

I walked on. I looked back over my shoulder and saw her huddled alone in her booth, weeping, face in hand. So I went back. "Let's have a coffee," thinking, To hell with my meeting, this is more important. "Or a drink. I can't leave you like this."

"No, no, you go on. I'm fine," she flapped a hand at me. "I am just so happy to see you. Thank you, thank you."

IT'S CURIOUS, but she is the only stranger to have mentioned the lack of breast. When I was in Malawi, staying with Katherine and Joshua who'd moved there to work at a mission hospital, I had expected questions. But the only incident was late one afternoon as I was walking down a narrow path through the mission tea plantation. Two teenage girls passed, then turned back and waved, giggling. We ran through the gamut of formal greetings in Chichewa then switched to English: "Hello, what's your name?" and so on. One of them pointed shyly at me then, putting a hand to her own right breast, she raised one finger. "One?" she asked, frowning. "Yes," I called back, chopping the air.

And that's all.

. . .

To them that are sick of the jaundice, honey seems
bitter; and to them that are bitten by a mad dog,
the water terrible; and to children, a little ball seems
a fine thing. And when then should I be angry?
MARCUS AURELIUS, *Meditations*

"**D**o you remember Martha?"
       I was taking a break outside the
studio, absorbed in the day's newspaper, not part of the general conversation. But they were talking about genetics and genetic testing, and I had started to half-listen. Martha had been a newsreader but had left a year after I'd started working at the radio.

"Her aunt and grandmother died of breast cancer," Xavier was saying, "so she went for genetic testing. I don't remember how many cases they said were genetically caused. A significant percentage anyway."

About ten percent, in the Netherlands at any rate, where roughly ten thousand women a year get breast cancer. I kept quiet.

"Well, she's going in next week to have both breasts amputated and a total hysterectomy."

"What?" I turned abruptly, horrified, joining in.

"Don't be so shocked." Teresa put a hand on my arm. "You'd have done that yourself if you'd known you were liable to cancer."

"I would not! It's absurd." I didn't care that this hadn't been my conversation in the first place. "Totally stupid. She might just as well *have* cancer if she's going to get rid of perfectly healthy breasts and womb and ovaries. She can only be thirty or so."

"Thirty-four," Xavier said.

"It's mad! She's blocking off life!"

There was a long silence. Xavier got up. "I'll fetch us some coffee, shall I?"

I got up too, I had to move.

"I'll come with you."

"A one-four for me, please," Teresa said.

"Anyone else?" asked Xavier.

"A two."

"And?"

"Nothing, just two, decaf."

"And mine's a four-two-three," called Paul as we turned to go.

"A one-four, two, four-two-three," muttered Xavier as the doors whooshed open and we walked down to the coffee machine. "Paul once tried to add up the number of permutations in the machine. He gave up at two hundred and eighty-four."

"I'm not surprised," I said grumpily, and pressed one-four. Black coffee spurted out into the plastic beaker, espresso with medium-high sugar.

"Four-two-three," prompted Xavier.

Four, three, my finger slipped. "Oh!" I exploded. It was so frustrating. Quickly I pressed the cancel button.

"Come on, let me do it. What's yours?"

"Does it matter?" I said. "All these options. They all taste horrid anyway."

"Hey, come on, it's only a machine."

"I know. That isn't what's bugging me though, it's that genetic stuff."

"Don't let it get to you. The woman's just being sensible." Xavier passed me the first cup.

"Sensible!" I stiffened. "Imagine wanting to cut things off that are healthy! Imagine having yourself mutilated just in case. I'm not upset, I'm cross."

"You think she should wait till she has cancer?"

"Yes. She might as well."

"Surely you can understand someone wanting to prevent that."

"No, I can't. Not at this sort of price."

"I think she's right." His voice had cooled. "I wish Mother had had the same chance."

His mother, too. Cancer seemed to be becoming commonplace.

ENJOYING A GLASS of wine on a terrace, waiting for Simon to turn up on one of his forays into town, my face tilted to the sun, I was approached by a man jangling a tin: research into breast cancer.

I shook my head.

He was startled: given what he must have noticed beneath my snugly fitting T-shirt, he must have thought I'd be a predictable easy touch. Not believing me, he presented the tin again.

Simon turned up just then. He waited a few seconds, then dropped a coin in himself and pulled up a chair. "Not like you not to give," he commented.

I winced. "Breast cancer's a fashionable cause so it attracts money that surely could be used better elsewhere," I said pompously.

"You don't think it should be a priority?"

"No. And if I can't say that, who can?"

I had benefited from a surgeon's skill, not from breast cancer research; Fanny Burney had benefited likewise as long ago as 1811—without anesthesia—and lived to write the tale. The other important thing I'd been given was time from doctors and nurses, hard-pressed hospital staff. "If it was money to train more nurses for cancer care, or for any nursing, come to that," I said, "I'd have paid." I'd have emptied my purse.

"Uh-huh." Simon nodded and changed the subject. "How about a game of pool?"

I got up to go inside with him, a little reluctant to leave the late-afternoon sunlight.

"Shall I order you more wine?" he asked.

"What are you having?"

"Tea," he said.

"Tea?" I stared at him. "At this hour—you? Then I'll have tea too. Why aren't you having beer?"

"I've been peeing a lot. No big deal. But Alex insisted I go to see her doctor."

"And?"

"And nothing. She said I was probably drinking too much beer and coffee and tea and I should lay off for awhile," he said.

"Right. So it's tea now."

"Hardly counts." He took the tea bag from its envelope and introduced it for only a couple of seconds to the hot water in his tea glass. "Anyway, it doesn't seem to make a difference. There's nothing the matter. It's just age," and he laughed. "Here, get playing." He passed me a cue. "By the way, we've decided to throw a party in three weeks' time, on the twenty-first. It's Alex's idea, to celebrate the anniversary of when we met. Will you come? We'd like you to."

"I'd love to," I said, neatly potting a ball.

*Do not seek death; death will find you. But seek
the road which makes death a fulfilment. In the last
analysis, it is our conception of death which decides
our answers to all the questions that life puts to us.*
DAG HAMMARSKJÖLD, *Markings*

Another intense bout of cancerchondria hit. Months had gone by without, then I fell and broke a rib and my wrist, the first bones I'd ever broken. When they were mended, I wondered about my liver.

"It feels funny here." I pressed the lump where my liver was. "I have a dull ache there all the time."

My doctor felt too, pressing gently.

"It could be the end of a floating rib, couldn't it?" I pleaded.

But he was taking no more chances, and sent me off for an X ray.

It was indeed my floating rib. But it took a week to find out. "I shan't be back," I told the doctor when he gave me the result. "No more false alarms."

"Good." We shook hands on it.

That was the day of Simon and Alex's party and I went down for it.

I was light-headed with joy and alcohol, celebrating, enjoying myself. When the other guests had left—it was too late to go home so I was staying the night—Simon, Alex, and I had a last glass of wine or two. I abandoned reserve and was voluble about how good life was, voluble about how critical liver secondaries would have been, garrulous about how cancer was becoming commonplace, unimportant in the vast scheme of things, mocking about my cancerchondria, swearing it would not recur.

They too were flushed with wine and excitement. The conversation moved on to the guests.

"I don't know what you saw in her," said Alex of Simon's ex-wife, who'd been there too.

Simon shrugged good-naturedly.

Alex looked at me for support.

Stupidly, I didn't give it. "She's OK," I said. First mistake. "Really?"

"She can be good company, and she was warm and generous to me. After all, Simon wasn't long divorced when we started our affair. She's not really my type," I added, "nor I hers, but we got on fine."

I wasn't reading the signals and there was no stopping me.

"Did you?"

"Sure. After all, if Simon—if anyone you're fond of—has been close to someone, or gets close to someone, you want to get on with them too, don't you?"

There was no stopping my honesty. "You don't want to lose contact, do you?" Second mistake.

Simon gave me a big hug before I camped down on their floor for the night. I left early in the morning before they were up and didn't see them. Remembering only the fun of the previous evening, I thought no more of what I had said.

HE RANG ME two days later. Back off, he warned. They'd had a scene that night, Alex upset by what I'd said about friendship. She claimed that I was manipulative and that I didn't really like her. He understood what I meant, and I was right, he said, but she approaches things differently, she isn't so analytical. Don't ring; I'll ring you. Give it a month or so.

It was like being punched. I wept. Unwittingly, I'd given her the opportunity she must have been looking for. Even then, before I knew what was to come, I realized that.

·　　·　　·

*Cancer is the quintessential disease of ageing. The
prime risk factor for cancer is age. Environmental
risk factors, such as cigarette smoking, work in part
because they accelerate the ageing process.*

MATT RIDLEY, *Genome*

Reading the paper over breakfast, I came to an article proposing that smokers pay a premium toward their health care when they get cancer. Why single them out? Should the overweight who develop diabetes pay toward their treatment? What about lovers of rich food whose arteries clog up? How far should you watch your health, how much should we protect ourselves from life? If you don't climb mountains, you might not fall and break a leg, or worse; if you don't fly, you might not get deep vein thrombosis. Too many sexual partners can lead to cervical cancer. Where does it stop? Living has consequences. I'd never smoked, though Simon did.

I took another bite of hot toast, butter melted into it.

I didn't know what my breast cancer was a consequence of: not having had children? Probably. It hadn't been genetic at any rate: that only applied if you got it before the menopause. Nor was it the result of HRT, which I'd never bothered with.

The phone rang. Simon. It was only a week after that last phone call.

"Remember I told you I was peeing a lot?"

I thought back. "Mmm?"

"I got fed up and went for a second opinion. They're doing tests."

I gulped down my mouthful of toast and concentrated. "What for?"

"Prostate."

"What exactly are the tests for?" I asked cautiously.

"Cancer."

"Bloody hell!" How could Simon go and get cancer?

I could hear plates clinking in the background. He and I were the same age, just fifty. My stomach clenched. "When will you hear the results?"

"On the tenth." He sounded bleak. "I've got to go."

"Shall I come over?"

"No, it's OK."

"I'll ring on the tenth then. I'll be thinking of you . . . " but he had hung up.

I chucked the toast. Then I rang Katherine and Joshua, my doctor friends. I thought they might know more.

"It's a good one to sort out, prostate cancer, as long as it's caught in time. Has it been?"

"I don't know." The conversation with Simon had been so brief. I'd been abrupt from the shock, he, I suppose, from being upset.

He'd want me around. I could help, couldn't I? He had been there for me. Of course he had Alex now, and she'd go to hospital with him and things—but he might want to see me too, mightn't he?

It was too soon after the upset with Alex to go over. But I had to do something. I rang a childhood friend of Simon's who saw him once a week, and asked him to give Simon a really good bottle of wine, champagne maybe, from me; it had played such a part when I'd been diagnosed. The friend sounded startled, but agreed.

It was difficult to fall asleep. Difficult not to follow my instincts and rush over. I closed the curtains, opened them. Turned on the light and read about prostate cancer in a book I had once had to write a synopsis for. Turned it off, opened the window wider, opened the curtain. Fell asleep at last.

I jerked awake. A bomb had gone off.

Or so I thought. I lay still, listening. No sounds of alarm started up from the houses and flats behind. No lights went on as I'd expected. I turned over to go back to sleep then changed my mind. I'd go to the loo first.

I went sleepily downstairs, turning on lights as I went. I wandered first into the kitchen at the back, just in case I could spot anything odd outside. Nothing. In the narrow hallway, opening the door to the loo, I paused. The door to my office in front, an old Victorian shop with a huge plate-glass window, was ahead of me. I pushed it open.

Half the window was gone, scattered across the high counter where I piled manuscripts and books, in glinting heaps on the desk at the window where I sat to translate. My faithful old typewriter, kept in case of computer break-down, was gone; they must have thought it was a laptop. Papers fluttered in the breeze from the hole. A square gray paving stone squatted on the floor amid shards of glass.

I had to wait in there till the police came, till a man came to patch up the window, till I had cleared the glass out from every corner and paper I could find, till dawn broke and it was at last safe to go back upstairs.

Later that morning, four men came to replace the whole sheet of plate glass. Then, bleary-eyed, I sat down to try to finish translating a piece before the deadline. On the pavement right outside the window, a dog squatted.

I tapped with my pen on the glass to put him off. His eyes rolled, but he stayed awkwardly hunched and began to crap. I waved my arms at him.

His owner hove into view: bleached hair piled high, scarlet lipstick flashing. "Is there a problem?" she snarled.

"Well, yes, look."

She looked, and then turned back to me.

"Please would you clear it up when he's done?" I asked through the glass.

"What the hell is that to do with you? Why should I? What do you think the council's for?"

I frowned.

"Look, lady, what's your game?" She was shouting now.

Don't make eye contact, I told myself. Head down, I returned to my translation and wrote gobbledygook, trying not to tremble.

She came to the window and stood in front of me on the other side. "You got anything to say, you come out here and say it," she screamed.

I scribbled on.

She spread her arms wide, blocking out the light. "Next time I come past here, I'll have someone with me!" Her spittle hit the glass. "Look at me, damn you!"

I looked.

She drew a finger across her throat, so viciously that it left a red mark. "That's what'll happen next time." And she strode off triumphantly.

It was difficult trying to sit still after all that. Still quivering, I took out my bicycle and set off for the market, plastic bag and wallet in the saddlebag.

A cyclist overtook me at the lights, so close I wobbled. When I stopped at my favorite fruit stall, the bag was gone and the wallet with it.

I went to the bank. When I came out, two drivers were having a row. One had a gun in his hand.

SIMON'S CANCER hadn't been caught in time. He rang me a few days later. It was already advanced, in his collarbone and spine.

Doth any man offend? It is against himself
that he doth offend: why should it trouble thee?
MARCUS AURELIUS, *Meditations*

"Where have you been?"
"What do you mean, where have I been? I've been here," Simon answered.

I was irritated at the tone of his voice. "Why didn't you ring back then? Did you get my letter? I've been trying to reach you for days," ever since the brief note he'd sent to say they were giving him a year, maybe a bit more. "I've left hundreds of messages on Alex's answering machine."

Pause. "Really?"

"Well—four then."

"Alex must have forgotten to tell me," he said. "She's been very busy."

"Oh, right. Good." But Simon used to tease Alex openly about not having enough to do and why didn't she get a job, she was perfectly capable.

"Anyway, you've got me now," he said.

"How's the hormone treatment going?"

"The hot flashes are a pain," he grumbled, "and I've put on weight. Now I know what women have to go through. Funny that, us both being on hormones. How are you?"

"I'm fine. Missing you," I said promptly. "Come and see me. Or I'll come down to you. How about next Saturday?"

"I'll check with Alex." He sounded distracted. "Look, I've got to go. I'll ring you." He cut the connection.

I put the phone down slowly. What was happening to us? He'd talked to me as if I was little more than an acquaintance.

In desperation, I rang the friend. It was only as we were talking that I understood how stupid I'd been, making assumptions, sending wine, champagne. Simon-with-Alex didn't necessarily react as Simon-before.

I had been told to watch my words. Now I had to watch my actions too. I felt adrift in a cold, clammy sea, in an unfamiliar current, spontaneity gone, lost forever. I wept.

There was a cooling. An ice age, if you prefer. Alex wanted me nowhere near.

How could I have been so crass?

Love is strong as death; jealousy as cruel
as the grave: the coals thereof are coals
of fire, which hath a most vehement flame.

SONG OF SOLOMON

One morning in a café, correcting a translation about taboos, I looked up to see that the breast-screening caravan had arrived and was squatting the length of the short quayside, a rectangular white toad. Its two windows stared out blankly. No one was going up the metal ladder to it, or down.

The day I'd gone up that short ladder it had been sunny, not windswept as today—and I had indeed said nothing of my suspicions, not when I stood there, flesh squashed between cold metal plates, not when they sent me out into the warm spring day, not when I heard nothing from the unit or my GP. I hadn't wanted to speak. I was happy to be reassured. Which makes me and my silence as complicit in the late diagnosis as the screening system. Which, as my doctor told me later, is not infallible; it's just that it picks up some cancers that mightn't be picked up otherwise. They tell you that now, sometimes.

LIKE ME, Simon had been diagnosed late.

At least my situation had been clear cut. The tumors were removed surgically and then there was tamoxifen. With Simon, it was hormone treatment and radiation, no operation. He'd put himself on mistletoe too, but it only made him feel worse and he stopped it.

Simon had said it was all right to phone now, about once a fortnight. But I usually got the answering machine and Alex's voice. Marie said she got it quite often too. On the rare occasion that I got Simon on the line, it was to hear a tirade. His words tumbled over themselves, reciting a minute medical report, details of PSA levels, hot spots, the latest trial he'd heard of and signed up for, all delivered in angry passion. I heard, I listened, I was noncommittal. His bitterness at the cancer shocked me. He blamed the first doctor who'd failed to diagnose it in time. But his anger was taking him nowhere; he couldn't turn back the clock.

And what do you do with another's anger, other than listen and sympathize? I could not enter into it. I didn't know this Simon. I had to be careful about what I said, doubly careful because of Alex, careful not to criticize decisions they had made together. My views on treatment would not be relevant to him. His cancer was different from mine, there is no typical cancer patient. Every cancer is a little different from every other, every victim copes with it differently.

If only I'd been able to see him face-to-face, it would have been all right; we could have talked about his anger, about death, about fear, and about other things, ordinary everyday things. And if I could see Alex, I could talk things through, clear the air, defend myself. But every time I arranged to go there, the date was canceled by Alex through a friend or on my answering machine, never direct, and always with a reason so plausible that I wanted to believe it.

Four months passed. Marie rang me constantly with detailed news of him, as did Connie; they saw him, though never, they told me, on their own—Alex always stayed in the room. She told Marie once that I'd said I didn't like her, and smiled skeptically when Marie said nonsense—although it was becoming true. My cancer was apparently a black mark too, yet another link between Simon and me that she couldn't share. She didn't want a cancer club, she told Marie. The irony was that my attitude to my own cancer actually inhibited me with Simon. On the few occasions we did speak on the phone, when he asked my opinion, I felt unable to contribute. But the comment about the cancer club gave a bit of comfort. Maybe sending the wine hadn't been so important after all, or what I'd said about friendship. Or maybe it had. Maybe all the time she'd been waiting for an excuse to shut me out, and my stupidity had given it to her. Oh, but how would I ever know without asking, and how could I ask unless I saw him?

It was tough for Alex. Of course it was: two months was all they'd had living together before he'd been diagnosed.

The weeks went by, months. Marie tried to mediate. She set up a time for me to go. She was sure I was being paranoid, of course he would see me this time. Write a note, she said, just to say when you're going; don't ask.

Alex rang up and canceled through Marie: he was tired, she said, from the last bout of palliative radiation. But I knew from Connie that she and Peter had been only the day before.

Two days later, after weeks of silence, Simon rang. He was calmer. We had a halfway decent conversation, I careful not to rock any boat. Until the end. I had to know: "Am I right in thinking I've become persona non grata?"

Silence. Then, "How about if I tell you that Alex is out all morning? When she comes back," he said dully, "she'll check the numbers I've rung."

"And?"

"There'll be a scene."

Can the dying be possessed?

A long life is not a question of years. A man
without memories might reach the age of a hundred
and feel that his life had been a brief one.
GRAHAM GREENE, *Travels with My Aunt*

What do you do with your memories?

When they come welling up, do you go into them, relive them, examine them, or do you detach yourself, walk away?

What do you do when a piece of music plays that played when you fell in love, or when your brother died? What do you do? Do you listen to it again?

Do you read all those letters you've kept from years before, or do you throw them away?

How do other people cope?

Tears leaked through my eyelids and dribbled onto the pillow.

I went round and round in circles.

I needed to talk to Simon, just once, if only about what we had shared. It no longer felt so important to sort out the misunderstandings; it was too late for that. This not seeing him was dreadful.

I couldn't. Alex didn't want him ringing. He wouldn't withstand her. She was being good to him. Those were the facts. Those I understood. But what harm did she think I could do? I could not believe in such small-spiritedness, such possessiveness.

Once I was with a friend when he died in hospital of AIDS. His lover wouldn't face being with him at the end, so it was up to me. You don't want to let anyone die alone, do you? On the Tuesday he stopped being able to speak, but he could still hear and communicate with his eyes and hands. On the Wednesday he was half-conscious, half-dozing. His breathing was faltering. For awhile he struggled. It was a beautiful night, clear, frosty, stars sparkling. I sat holding his hand. His eyes were fixed on me, and I could see some fear in them, for the first time. I told him about the night and felt him begin to relax. "Close your eyes," I told him. "Close your eyes and I'll sing the blessing to you. And let go. Just let go. It's all right."

He closed his eyes.

"The Lord bless you and keep you," I sang, "the Lord make His face to shine upon you and be gracious unto you.

The Lord lift up His countenance upon you and give you peace. Amen."

A thin trickle of blood slipped out of his mouth onto the pillow. His fingers relaxed in mine. He was gone. One moment his spirit was there, the next not. Simple.

IF I RANG Simon, I got the answering machine.

I wrote him a letter. I had to, it was all that was left to me. If I couldn't see him, I had to tell him how important he had been to me, as lover and as friend. I phrased it carefully, not a word too many, diplomatically and truthfully. I finished by saying that if he ever did want to see me, I would be there.

It made no difference.

Simon died. I never saw him again. He died after a battle with cancer. A cliché but, in his case, true. No acceptance for him, only that corrosive anger.

He grabbed at everything on offer, he volunteered for trials, was turned down, and again. He could not accept. It was wretched. He was wretched.

He died.

I went to the funeral. Alex wanted no one but herself at the graveside. I was sick as a dog all the way back on the train. Simon's funeral. I barely remember it.

God shall wipe away all tears from their eyes;
and there shall be no more death, neither sorrow,
nor crying, neither shall there be any more pain:
for the former things are passed away.

REVELATION

With fewer people going to priests and ministers for comfort and counseling, grief counseling is an ever-growing industry. I heard a woman on the radio, speaking of her experiences: there are considered to be five steps of grief. She was informed by her counselor that she wasn't grieving "properly" because she hadn't taken the steps, one at a time, and in the prescribed order, rigidly.

Curiously, now that it was over I just felt calm. My frustration fell away. I'd kept the letters Simon had sent when we'd fallen in love and I read them now, not having looked at them for years. They helped me to reclaim the Simon I had known and loved, they and my friends, mine and his. Also the fact that he'd rung me only two days before he died, relaxed, almost his old self, though his voice was faint. Alex had gone out. "I'm hanging on for grim death," he'd said; when he realized his mistake, he laughed, and the laughter had turned to coughing.

It was as it was. All I could do now was pray for peace for Simon.

Lying awake again one night, I brooded on after-death. In my mind, I talked to him about it. Hell had just been sort of abolished by the Anglican synod, I'd heard on the BBC. Not that it had ever seemed likely to me, except as a symbol or metaphor both for no one remembering you when you've gone and for suffering here on earth. For those reasons alone, it's a useful concept. But then what about Heaven?

I don't fancy a Christian heaven, at least not the way it's presented in *Revelation* and in so many hymns. So noisy with its hosts of angels and saints blinding you with the brilliant white and gold of their robes, deafening you with their constant singing, clashing of cymbals, blowing of trumpets, in a city of golden mansions where the only animals are weird, apocryphal ones. Very urban and unlikely. The impression I have of the Islamic paradise sounds far

more appealing: green meadows, space, sunshine, time, bab-
bling brooks, birdsong, and butterflies. It's more in tune
with the spirit of the thing. "Be still and know that I am
God." How can you do that in the noisy Christian version?

The Islamic vision comes closer to how I imagine it will
be: a metaphysical embrace, beyond emotion, beyond measure, beyond time, beyond worldly understanding. Christian
mysticism has that too, and Buddhism and Hinduism.
Total absence, total presence, total love.

Anyway, it's all metaphor. I already have an inkling of
the embrace. I'm not afraid of death. Simon had been. Who
was I to say if religion, any religion, might have helped?

No man dies before his hour. The time you
leave behind was no more yours than that which
was before your birth, and concerns you no more.
MICHEL DE MONTAIGNE, *Essays*

They make it difficult for you to accept a cancerous death nowadays. Even, or so some see it, to accept death itself. Refuse a transplant and you're being irresponsible.

When I'm dead, I hope no one says I died after a long battle with cancer. Anyway, I'm not battling, and I'm not going to. I accept it. The way Simon had battled with his cancer only strengthened my own resolve. Apparently you're meant to take on treatment, however debilitating and nasty, in the hope that something else will come along before you reach the end of the road. Or they create embryos for your benefit. I have a vision of lines of petri dishes with pink tadpole-beings in them, being kept alive, while needles harvest their stem cells so that people like me can cheat death. Cannibalism by any other name, surely? And the ever more sophisticated medical interventions seem indecent: we already live far, far longer than most of the rest of the world.

I don't want anything that'll make me more ill in my last days; I don't see the point in gaining an extra year. I'd rather enjoy what I have. I'd rather have good nursing at the end, be sure that I won't die alone.

Will I stick to this if the cancer spreads? There's no knowing in advance how you'll react, though I hope I do.

And what about telling people? Part of me thinks not. It slipped out spontaneously first time round. "How are you?" they'd ask casually, and I'd answer, unable to do otherwise. But then there was the focus of an operation which made it easier for everyone. If it spreads further, will I do as I imagine now? I'd want friends to share in my dying, and yet how awful if the "How are you?" became loaded each time and I turned into little more than a sum of reactions to that question: cancer and me inseparable for ever. Friends can't win. Of course they'll ask. It's the practical help that's needed, though, the suggestion that you leave the dinner table and go to bed because they've noticed you're looking tired, the invitation to come and stay.

No one said relationships and dying would be easy.

Stir up thy mind, and recall thy wits again
from thy natural dreams and visions, and when
thou art perfectly awoken, and canst perceive that
they were but dreams that troubled thee, as one
newly awakened out of another kind of sleep look
upon these worldly things with the same mind as
thou didst upon those, that thou sawest in thy sleep.
MARCUS AURELIUS, *Meditations*

Last night my father tried to kill me. In my dream I was on top of a cliff in brilliant sunshine. It was soft and powdery, and the surface glared white in the sun. The cliff dropped below me to sea so deep it was almost black. I gazed down. Suddenly I realized that I was standing on an outcropping, thin and slightly sloping. No sooner had I realized this than the outcropping began to crumble gently at the edge. I inched back up the slope, eyes fixed on the drop, terrible now. Each step was a struggle as the surface turned into powder and slid beneath my feet, but I made tense, slow progress.

I stopped, blocked, my shoulders suddenly grasped by my father. He was standing behind me pointing to something below, I couldn't see what, and talking excitedly, I couldn't hear what. In his enthusiasm, he stopped me from going back further. The cliff went on sliding, crumbling. It would give way under my feet unless I moved. I would fall to my death.

I sensed another man come up behind my father. He released his hands from my shoulders. He pulled me to safety.

That nightmare did it. I woke up, shivering, ran to the lavatory and threw up.

I made myself tea and sat at the open window at the back overlooking the gardens and listened. Birds squawked and trilled. Steam billowed from bathroom windows, voices were raised, someone started to whistle. In the breeze, the curtain brushed my cheek.

I got dressed and went for a walk along the river. The trees were clouds of white blossom, I breathed in the scent of daffodils and new grass. A mongrel bounded up, tail wagging, and licked my hand vigorously.

A switch flicked in my mind. My perspective on life rushed back in.

I stopped at a café. The waiter, yawning, brought me a croissant and a bowl of milky coffee. I tore at the croissant and licked the buttery flakes off my fingers. Ordered more. The waiter put on reggae music. The café cat jumped on my lap, and I let it stay there while I gazed out at the street and the river beyond, foot tapping.

If this was all, it was enough.

·   ·   ·

Love is not changed by death and
nothing is lost, and all in the end is harvest.
JULIAN OF NORWICH

That was six months ago. Life is still sweet.

A colleague today over lunch in the radio canteen said: "Don't you ever feel you're living with a time bomb?"

I shake my head. Three years on, two years of tamoxifen to go, I sometimes think about cancer and wonder, but not often, not now.

ACKNOWLEDGMENTS

A big thank-you to my doctor and the surgeons and nurses at the hospital for their excellent treatment, and to my dear family, friends, and colleagues for care, humor, generosity, and loving kindness.

I am grateful to the Carcanet Press for permission to reproduce Robert Graves's "Flying Crooked."

J an Michael was born in Yorkshire and now lives in Amsterdam, where she works as a writer and literary agent. She has written both children's books and four novels, including *The Lost Lover* and *Amsterdam Blues*.